FURTHEST NORTH

AN EPIC ADVENTURE ROWING THE ARCTIC TO A POLE POSITION

BY ROD MACRAE

To Michael
Dare to win
[signature]

Published by:
Frozen World Publishing
Couching House,
Watlington,
Oxfordshire, Great Britain
OX49 5PX

ISBN: 978-0-9571056-0-7
© 2011 Rod Macrae/Frozen World Publishing

© 2011 Photographs and illustrations were generously provided by members of the crew & support team. They retain copyright and their images published in this book cannot be reproduced or re-printed without their permission.
Satellite images on p15 & p46: RADARSAT-2 Data and Products © MacDONALD DETTWILER AND ASSOCIATES LTD (2011).
All rights reserved. RADARSAT is an official marque of the Canadian Space Agency.
Other images courtesty of Michael Hughes Photography (www.michaelhughesphoto.com)

Printed in the UK

DEDICATION

This book is dedicated to the memory of twelve passengers who lost their lives and to the survivors of the First Air Boeing 737 plane crash at Resolute Bay on August 20th 2011.

FOREWARD

At the National Maritime Museum in Greenwich, you can almost feel the presence of people who, in a far tougher age than our own, explored what were then msyterious parts of our planet. Their expeditions were voyages into the unknown. They were often epic arduous journeys of discovery and many who set out on them paid a high price in attempting to further the boundaries of knowledge. Some never returned.

Amongst the exhibits at the museum there is a chart from the early 1900s. It shows only a blank space in the area we crossed in the Old Pulteney Row To The Pole expedition in 2011.

Today the physical geography of the Arctic region is known. The islands of the Canadian archipelago have names and their features have been recorded. Although not so intensively surveyed as some other parts of our planet, we do know a lot about the top of the world. And yet, there is still a call for more physical exploration. However, the reasons are different from those which motivated our predecessors. This remote place continues to draw scientists to study it and adventurers seeking the ultimate test, pitting themselves against its harsh conditions.

It is true that the Old Pulteney Row To The Pole was not primarily scientific although one of the crew, Dave Mans, captured data for scientists at the National Oceanography Centre at Southampton University. It was first and foremost a physical endeavour. We were seeking to row our boat high into the Arctic, where no oarsmen had ever been before. However, it was only possible because of striking and troubling changes to the environment of this fragile polar region.

The area we rowed into was, until recent years, covered by floating sea ice year-round. The huge retreat of sea ice over recent decades is a major phenomenon and is being keenly studied by oceanographers and climate scientists seeking to understand the consequences of global warming. When the idea for the expedition first came to me I recognised that, by making our attempt, we could highlight the threat of climate change.

I had, in 1996, been part of an expedition which helped to certify the position of the Magnetic North Pole. Its position has since become a recognised end point for numerous Arctic adventures over the ice and my own Polar Race competitors have it as their objective. My thinking was that rowing there in summer, a journey I was frequently told was impossible, would be a graphic demonstration of the scale of the changes occurring in this frozen wilderness. Our story would, for the majority of people, be a simpler one to absorb than any scientific findings could ever be. Surely, anyone reading about a crew rowing to a pole position, would easily understand that something serious must be happening to our climate.

As a maritime adventurer, the appeal of the expedition was its combination of rowing and polar challenges. I knew the people with the skills and, if it was possible, I was confident they would be the ones capable of proving it.

Most of all, it was a journey which connected to some of my own personal heroes. Sir James Clark Ross was the first to locate the position of the Magnetic North Pole in 1831, and Sir Ernest Shackleton undertook one of history's greatest feats of endurance in 1916. Shackleton led his crew on an 800 mile journey to safety in open boats. The *James Caird* crossed the Southern Ocean from Elephant Island to South Georgia after Shackleton's ship Endurance was crushed by ice in Antarctica. In getting his boat to Elephant Island he had to row and drag them across the ice. It was the last time an expedition rowed any distance in either polar region.

On August 25th 2011 our rowing boat *Old Pulteney* completed its journey. Against the odds we had succeeded in an epic row. The voyage itself lasted just four weeks, but to me it was the culmination of four years of planning. This book tells the story of how we did it.

Jock Wishart

THE EXPEDITION PHOTOGRAPHERS

This book features photographs capturing every step of the journey taken on the *Old Pulteney Row To The Pole* expedition. Most are by members of the support team and crew of the *Old Pulteney*. Their images have enabled *Furthest North* to tell the story of their remarkable journey. Many of the images in this book were taken using Fujifilm Finepix XP30. The cameras allowed the crew to take photographs in the toughest conditions. Billy Gammon says: "We leapt into the water with our dry suits on, rowed on the open deck and ventured onto the ice carrying the cameras everywhere. They were bumped and battered constantly, so it's amazing these cameras came out unscathed."

Mark Beaumont
Aside from rowing, Mark's main role on the expedition was as a documentary-maker for the BBC. His additional skill with a stills camera has produced some of this books most remarkable images. An experienced adventurer, Mark has previously recorded his own solo expeditions on camera when cycling around the world and from the far north to the far south of the Americas. *www.markbeaumontonline.com*

Tony Woodford
Tony has been photographing expeditions in the Arctic for more than 10 years and has worked with Jock Wishart on numerous adventures based in Resolute. For the *Old Pulteney Row To The Pole* he was part of the support boat crew which tracked the *Old Pulteney* during its first 7 days after leaving Resolute Bay, giving him a perfect platform for his photography. *www.arcticmonkey.co.uk*

Richard Webster
Richard was part of the operations team in Resolute. He captured images of the final preparations. Richard is an experienced wildlife photographer combining his life as a zoologist with his technical skills behind the lens. *www.websterswildshots.com*

Billy Gammon
Along with Mark Beaumont, Billy's photography forms part of the visual record of the expedition captured by the crew themselves. Without professing to have specialist skills with a camera, Billy has nevertheless helped to provide a unique insight into the crew's experiences on their voyage.

INTRODUCTION

At Resolute Bay, high in the Canadian Arctic, the first glimmer of light on the horizon brings with it the expedition season. It is short – lasting only from late February until early May. Into Resolute, a tiny hamlet of few than 200 people, comes a sudden influx of migrants: explorers passing through on their way out to their polar adventures. They're already in one of the most remote places on Earth and about to experience the unforgiving conditions that characterise the large white area at the top of world.

"What are you going to do next Jock? Row to the North Pole!"

However, scientists have been observing major changes to this vast global feature. The extent of the Arctic ice has declined over the last 30 years. In both winter and summer, the area of ice has shrunk. Following this observation has come a realisation that climate change has a more marked impact at both Poles, and that the consequences are far-reaching. Despite this apparent warming, for the adventure community the thermometer still continues to plummet to its unimaginable lows each winter, drawing them north. Spring brings rapidly longer days, quickly extending to 24-hour daylight, whilst the ice remains thick and stable until a colossal melt begins, making exploration on a frozen ocean impossible after mid-May.

In April 2007 Jock Wishart was amongst this seasonal crowd at the South Camp Inn with competitors he had brought to the Arctic for the Polar Race. With a support team based in Resolute, Jock had encouraged and guided the competitors to the end of the race, some 450 miles away off Ellef Ringnes Island on the edge the vast Arctic Ocean. Their precise destination was the 1996 Magnetic North Pole position, a dot on the map which Jock himself had helped to certify on an expedition some eleven years earlier.

Waiting for his racers to return to Resolute, Jock was getting bored. He carried a rowing machine from the hotel's gym onto the snow and began exercising in the extreme cold. It was -20 °C. "What are you going to do next Jock? Row to the North Pole!"

His colleague Chris Walker could not have known that his comment was to spark an idea which became the *Old Pulteney Row To The Pole*. "I couldn't get it out of my mind" Jock recalls. "On the plane heading south at the end of the trip I could see the ice was beginning to break up as it does every year at its more southerly extent. Maybe, I thought, just maybe....."

Above: May 3rd 2007. *The Eureka moment - Jock on a rowing machine in Resolute.* **Opposite:** *Sea ice melts each summer in the Arctic.*

Months later in his office, Jock had maps of the Arctic spread across the floor. The latest bulletin from the US National Snow and Ice Data Centre had reported that the seasonal ice melt in the Arctic had reached a record low.

The areas newly shown as mostly open water suggested it was conceivable to attempt a row to the 1996 position of the Magnetic North Pole. Vast areas which had once been under year-round ice were now, to his eye, navigable much further north than he had imagined.

Within a short time some of the key elements of an expedition had been set in place. Ewan Angus, the Contoller of BBC Scotland, had suggested that a documentary programme of a row in the Arctic would make good television. An ice expert, Kim Partington, had begun studying the route a voyage would take and the first key crew member, Rob Sleep, had been approached. The *Row To The Pole* project had begun.

SHAPING THE MISSION

The hardest work in an expedition lies in its planning. Painstaking research is needed to assess the scale of the challenge. This expedition was, however, clearly different from others Jock had planned. It was going to be a voyage like no other.

"No one had rowed in polar waters in recent times, there was no blueprint" says Jock. "Charts had last been updated from land almost 50 years ago, and the waters had only just begun to be clear of ice in summer – almost like a whole new sea appearing out of nowhere. We would be taking our boat into these largely unknown waters in conditions that had never been experienced by oarsmen or sailors before."

With so little to guide them, the team had to anticipate the challenges they could face. All of the potential obstacles were assessed: currents, prevailing weather, and the amount of floating ice at each stage of the expedition.

There was one extra danger for this expedition: attacks from polar bears. The route was through the bears' wilderness habitat, making close encounters a near certainty. Narwhals were an unknown quantity too. Little is known about these strange marine mammals, and it was possible they would see the boat as a predator coming through their breeding grounds off the Grinnell Peninsula.

Jock explains: "From this first outline of the expedition, I was able to decide on the overall 'shape' and feel of the adventure. I now had a good idea how many people should be in the crew and of the technical specification for the boat itself."

PARTNERSHIP AND SPONSORS

In total, the expedition cost £500,000. The acquisition of Old Pulteney Single Malt Whisky as the Title Sponsor secured a partner whose funds allowed the major investment in the project to go ahead. In reality, this became a partnership with significantly more support in marketing and media relations.

Despite the punishing economic climate in 2008 onwards, additional sponsors were sought and secured. Billy Gammon drove the sponsorship programme, making more than 125 pitches. "I relied on finding partners who shared the dream and had the vision to see they would be part of something special. It is always easier to say 'no', but it takes courage to say 'yes'. Without our sponsors there would not have been an expedition and we are grateful to have secured such a strong portfolio of partners."

Equally important was saving money by securing kit, equipment and services at no cost or at a heavily reduced price in exchange for sponsorship rights.

From an expedition perspective, every sponsor was essential, and the value of these relationships cannot be underestimated. Ideas, encouragement and support came flooding in from all directions. Many others simply gave their time for free. They may not all have been recognised, but such contributions were highly appreciated.

"...every sponsor was essential, and the value of these relationships cannot be underestimated."

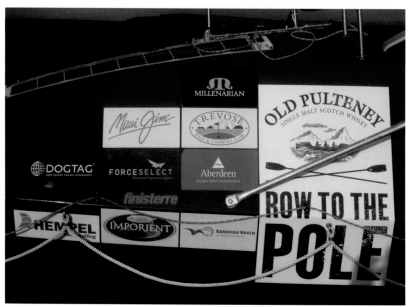

EXPEDITION SPONSORS

Old Pulteney Single Malt Whisky
Boisdale
Canadian North
DMS Technologies
Dogtag Insurance
Durham University
Finisterre
Force Select
Fujifilm
Hempel
Henri Lloyd
Henshaw Inflatables
Icebreaker
Imporient Tea
iMediasport
Jimmy Green Marine
LDC
Lewmar
Loudmouth Golf
Lyon Equipment
Macrae Media & Communication
Mactra
Marlec
Maui Jim
MDA
Millenarian
Ocean Safety
Ocean World
Palm
Polar Adventures
Raymarine
Rossiter Yachts
SEMS Aerosafe

South Camp Inn, Resolute
Southampton University
Trevose Golf & Country Club
Trimline
Yellowbrick

THE BOAT

The boat design was critical to the expedition. At first glance it would look like any other ocean rowing boat, with fore and aft sleeping cabins and a rowing deck between. However, there would need to be significant innovations to make her suitable for the Arctic.

"I knew we'd be facing fast-moving, broken, ice floes and that collisions were unavoidable" said Jock Wishart. "With a navigable route far from certain, I also knew we should anticipate having to haul the boat across large areas of ice. That meant the hull would have to be specially designed – and to be lightweight so that the crew had a chance of pulling her."

The boat required was a completely new class of vessel: an ice boat. Boat builders, designers and a sledge builder all contributed to its specifications. Hugh Welbourne suggested a 'cathedral hull' similar to those seen on large 20-paddle Chinese dragon boats. This concept was then taken up by Roger Daynes, who had built expedition sledges. Sledge runners were incorporated into the hull. All of this was pulled together by marine architect Peter Bosgraaf. For strength, the hull was to be built using a carbon/kevlar sheeting over marine ply on the outside, with kevlar only on the inside.

There was a nagging concern: how to get the boat out of water onto floating ice? The solution adopted was by master mariner John Page, and was based on an idea from the pit-lane of Formula One racing. At every pit stop tyres are changed using a fulcrum and lever device to lift the body of the car upwards. By adapting this simple principle, the boat could be fitted with rollers at the bow, under which metal poles could form runners that would get the aft of the vessel out the water.

As expedition leader, Jock Wishart's biggest headache lay in being able to get the boat from the specialist builders, Rossiter Yachts, at Christchurch, Dorset, on the south coast of England to Resolute Bay in Canada. With time already tight for the scheduled attempt to be made

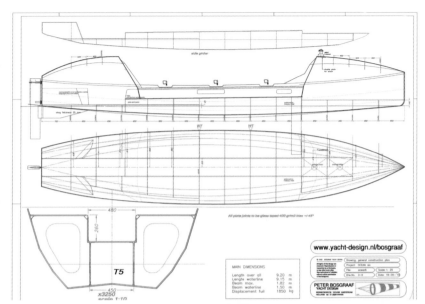

Above: Design drawings by Peter Bosgraaf.
Opposite: The boat under construction at Rossiter's in Christchurch

The boat required was a completely new class of vessel: an ice boat

in August 2011, the only option was to fly her on the last leg of the journey in a cargo plane. This immediately limited the size of the boat, and the space available for rowing positions and sleeping accommodation. Whatever its final size, the boat would need to be packed into the cargo hold of the aircraft which supply Resolute Bay from one of the Arctic North's main aviation hubs at Yellowknife, in Canada's Northwest Territories.

This transportation issue meant the boat would be 9.2 metres long, with three sculling positions. The ingenuity of Peter Bosgraaf's design meant that it was just possible to accommodate six crew, and all the equipment and provisions, for a totally self-sufficient voyage.

By July 2010 the unique ice boat hull was complete, and it was possible to see the Welbourne, Daynes and Bosgraaf collaboration had worked. The rowing positions, deck and cabin fittings were all completed and to keep the expedition's finances on track, marine supplies were willingly donated by supportive suppliers Lewmar (hatches and fittings), Hempel (formerly Blake Paints), Mactra (water maker) and Raymarine (instruments).

After three years of planning, the sketches and ideas had resulted in a magnificent boat. As it emerged from the Rossiter Yachts' boat yard in November 2010 for her sea trials the team was able to see the world's first ice rowing boat ready for trials.

Mark Delstanche was responsible for some ingenious modifications: "One of the distinguishing features was our lee board. We added it when we realised that winds and currents were going to make the boat track or drift. A centrally placed dagger board would not work because we'd be forever lifting it up to get the boat over ice or to avoid hitting underwater obstacles. In the end I solved the problem with a feature taken from a lot of wide-bottomed estuary boats, like Dutch barges. It's a board you can attach to either side of the boat and it prevents sideways movement. It worked a treat."

Top: *Mark Delstanche and Jock Wishart working on the boat;* *Bottom*: *Solar panels and Iridium communications uplink on the aft cabin roof;* *Opposite*: *on the River Thames at Ham.*

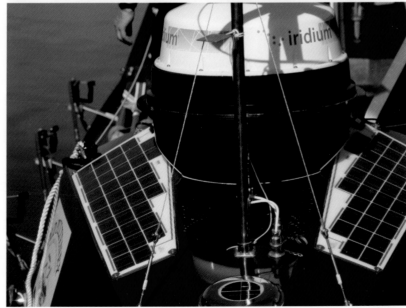

THE ROUTE

Satellite images of the Arctic can tell you a lot about the big picture. They show where the ice is and, to some extent, show the thickness of the ice at any time of year. There are regular reports from Environment Canada, the National Snow and Ice Data Centre and NASA in the United States as well as the European Space Agency. This widely available bank of images was used to decide on the route.

Looking at satellite photos showed how, over time, the extent of ice in both summer and winter had shrunk. Since satellite monitoring of sea ice began 30 years ago, its surface area has declined in summer by an average of 11.6 percent each decade. Significantly, for route planning, the images show the distribution and how this varied year by year. With a maximum of only five weeks to complete the exercise before the sea started freezing again, the 'window' was small. Besides, to Jock's dismay, the melt in 2009 and 2010 had been too late to make the attempt possible.

Leaving Resolute Bay, the route followed the southern coastline of Cornwallis Island to the Wellington Channel. According to the satellite images, most of this first section looked to be largely free of ice at its southern reaches every summer. However, there was still likely to be floating ice debris, even at the southern end of the Wellington Channel. Using a route that followed the coast of Devon Island, the ice would begin to be densely packed towards the Grinnell Peninsula. There, currents from several major channels were likely to push broken sea ice closely together. From this point, it was anticipated that the journey would be a game of cat and mouse, as ice borne south by currents would be blown around by the prevailing winds.

North of the Grinnell Peninsula there was also a far greater uncertainty of where, and how, the seasonal ice would melt in 2011. The ideal route would be a long direct crossing to the south west of Ellef Ringnes Island and then onwards along the island's coast towards Deer Bay and the 1996 position of the Magnetic North Pole.

"We had to try and anticipate which areas were most likely to be navigable. In reality none of our plans carried a cast iron guarantee" Jock Wishart explained. "The truth is we were plotting a journey that had so many variables, that it amounted to a theoretical route. At my most optimistic, I'd put our chances of success at about sixty percent, but there were times when the odds seemed much lower."

If the weather conditions did not help to break up the ice, or the melt in 2011 did not reach the west side of Ellef Ringnes Island, then the team would be forced to abandon the attempt with no real prospect of completing the voyage.

To improve the chances of success, it was realised detailed satellite images of the ice just ahead of the boat would be needed. This would allow the team to exploit wider leads of open water which might open up, enabling them to inch northwards during the final section of the route. Canadian company MDA were excited by the ambition of the expedition and agreed to supply this vital intelligence.

"It amounted to a theoretical route. I'd put our chances of success at about sixty percent, but there were times when the odds seemed much lower."

A satellite image of the expedition route taken by RADARSAT-2 in May 2011. The ice on the route is already beginning to melt and break up. Images captured by the satellite were provided by MDA throughout the expedition, giving the team strategically vital data about the conditions along their route.

Top: *Dave Mans at the Selection Day; Jock Wishart; Mark Beaumont;* **Middle:** *Rob Sleep; Contestants for the Pole Position working out at the Selection Day; Dave Mans who won the Pole Position competition;* **Bottom:** *Mark Delstanche; Billy Gammon; Crew Selection Day.*

CHOOSING THE CREW

Selecting the right people to join the expedition was not easy. When you are planning an Arctic expedition the most important thing is your crew. When Sir Ernest Shackleton was seeking his crew almost a century a go he made it clear what kind of people he needed – and pulled no punches:

> *"Men wanted for hazardous journey. Small wages, bitter cold, long months of complete darkness, constant danger, safe return doubtful, honour and recognition in case of success."*
>
> (Sir Ernest Shackleton's advertisement in The Times, 1915)

This expedition would not be as dangerous, but whoever accepted a place on the Old Pulteney would face a severe test of their mettle. Jock Wishart knew that only a few people would have the right combination of rowing prowess, temperament and other skills to be part of his team. Whoever was selected had to be part of a crew which would be entirely self-sufficient on the voyage.

"I'd recruited Rob Sleep first because he is so unflappable and, should anything happen to me, would be able to skipper the boat" Jock explains. "Then, as word spread about my plans, I began to get calls from people interested in the expedition."

Amongst those chosen from these enquiries were Mark Delstanche and Billy Gammon. Mark is a 'super yacht' captain, rower and adventurer. He had just returned from climbing Everest. Billy had skippered a crew through a successful crossing of the Indian Ocean. Mark became the 'make-it-happen' man, supervising the boat build and sharing in the navigational duties on the expedition. Billy, a Cornishman, had been living in New Zealand where he had been awarded a major Kiwi honour for his ocean rowing achievement. His professional skills in sponsorship and marketing made him ideal as the boat's communicator.

With three crew chosen, there were two places left. These would be taken by Mark Beaumont, nominated by the BBC to join the boat as their documentary film-maker. With space at a premium on the boat, it was agreed that whoever they asked to be on the expedition would also have to earn their keep as an oarsman. Mark's previous adventures had all been solo cycling expeditions. He had pedalled round the world and completed a major journey from the far North of America to the southern tip of South America. Both had been recorded to make highly popular TV programmes.

Whoever accepted a place on the Old Pulteney would face a severe test of their mettle.

The final place was taken by the winner of an open competition, the Old Pulteney Pole Position contest. Attracting 700 enquiries, Jock whittled down the applicants to 48 candidates who were invited to the Olympic Rowing Course at Dorney Lake, near Windsor. There, where the 2012 Olympic rowing competitions are to be staged, they undertook physchometric and physical tests. With a shortlist of eleven emerging, the last position was filled by Captain David Mans, a serving Army Officer with The Princess of Wales' Royal Regiment. Dave had previously rowed competitively at club level, and for the Army.

Like all the other crew, Dave Mans also had other talents and, with a degree in Oceanography, willingly took on the role of shaping the science programme.

Two other members of that shortlist, Lieut. Col. Justin Holt of the Royal Marines and British born Canadian resident Richard Webster, agreed to be travelling reserves and to run the Base Camp in Resolute.

TRAINING

Seven months before the Old Pulteney would be shipped across to Canada, the crew was finally able to start putting the boat through her paces. The crew had all been following a detailed programme of strength, conditioning and endurance training, putting in long hours in the gym, mostly on rowing machines.

As soon as the boat was sea worthy the crew began their ocean training, getting used to rowing together and understanding how the boat performed in the water.

As Billy Gammon describes: "Every weekend training session that passed, we'd get to know each other that little bit better. Putting the 'ice boat' through her paces was fantastic and we began to realise what an amazing vessel she was. I must admit, I quickly became very fond of her!"

Within the crew there were different skills as oarsmen. After trying different combinations in the three rowing positions, it was decided that Billy Gammon and Mark Beaumont would be in the 'engine room' in the second position, with the stroke seat occupied by Dave Mans and Mark Delstanche over the two alternating watches, while Rob Sleep and Jock would fit into the bow positions, which definitely suited shorter people!

Setting out from Christchurch, training usually involved heading out into the Solent to pit their wits against some challenging currents and tides.

To Jock these amounted to sea trials. "We learnt a lot about the boat each time and made improvements where necessary. We needed to know how fast the boat would go in typical sea conditions, despite having a sledge-like bottom. In fact, it turned out that we could manage a pretty decent 3.5 knots in an hour. We went exceedingly well upwind in up to 20 knots of headwind, thanks to the innovative lee board."

BON VOYAGE

With days to go before the boat was shipped to Canada, the Old Pulteney was named in what may seem like odd circumstances. Outside Boisdale's restaurant on Cabot Square at Canary Wharf, sponsors, family, friends and journalists gathered around the boat on its tow trailer.

Margaret Mary Clarke, Senior Brand Manager at Old Pulteney, tippled whisky over the bow. With the boat duly christened, Jock Wishart quoted a poem by a personal friend, international rugby player Andy Ripley who had died the previous year.

Dare we hope? We dare.
Can we hope? We can.
Should we hope? We must.
We must, because to do otherwise is to waste the most precious of
gifts, given so freely by God to all of us.
So when we do die, it will be with hope and it will be easy
and our hearts will not be broken.

(Andy Ripley, 10 June 2007, Athlone Friary)

Above and left (Clockwise): *Rowing off Weymouth; Mark Beaumont films a training row; Naming The Old Pulteney; Mark Delstanche, Billy Gammon and Jock Wishart on the oars.*

BOAT IN A BOX

Few expeditions start in a freight company's loading bay, but on June 17th 2011 Mark Delstanche was watching as the Old Pulteney was gently inched into a container at the Trade Freight International Terminal in Newark, Nottinghamshire, to begin her long journey to Resolute Bay.

Packed into the boat was a huge supply of equipment and clothing for the expedition. The 'boat in a box' left the UK from Liverpool, bound for Halifax, Nova Scotia, before being transferred onto a truck and taken by road to Yellowknife in northern Canada. It took four weeks to reach the airport at Yellowknife, where Mark Delstanche, Dave Mans and Tony Woodford met her in mid-July, to fly with her on a Buffalo transport plane for the final leg to Resolute.

Yellowknife was the last town where supplies could be sourced. The extra kit included satellite phones, biodegradable bags, emergency flares and some medical essentials, all of which were stowed into the holds of the boat before she was taken out of the container and into the cargo hold of the plane. If any of the boat's proportions had been inaccurate, she would not have fitted into the hold.

It was a tight squeeze, but the handling crew managed to manoeuvre the Old Pulteney into position and brace her for the flight. From the cock-pit of the plane there was a first glimpse of the endless Arctic wilderness below and the broken sea ice on the water.

When the plane touched down in Resolute, the boat had travelled 6,175 miles to reach the starting line for the expedition.

When the plane touched down in Resolute, the boat had travelled 6,175 miles to reach the starting line for the expedition.

Opposite: The Old Pulteney was packed into a container for transportation by ship, truck and cargo plane. Tony Woodford, Mark Delstanche and Dave Mans accompanied her from Yellowknife to Resolute Bay.

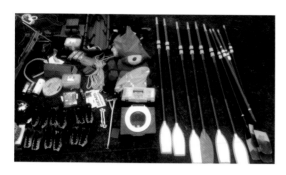

FINAL PREPARATIONS

A special atmosphere surrounds the final preparations for an expedition. There is an unmistakable excitement which is slowly overtaken by apprehension.

By July 23rd 2011 there were eleven people assembled. For all of them to have reached Resolute meant the start of the expedition. Kit had to be checked, tested, prepared and stowed, and the boat readied for action.

Resolute, at 74°41'N 094°52'W, is at the very end of a thin supply chain. A single cargo ship reaches it annually at the end of the summer. There was no time for replacements to be flown in for anything which had been overlooked, leaving improvisation as the only solution to problems. Like so many expeditions, The *Old Pulteney Row To The Pole* owes enormous thanks to Aziz Kheraj, who not only runs the South Camp Inn, but lends his expertise and local knowledge to solve countless problems.

Mark Delstanche, later joined by Jock and Rob Sleep, prepared *The Old Pulteney*. Every aspect required careful scrutiny to ensure it was in full working order. Attention to detail was everything.

The rest of the team focused on other details. Richard Webster and Justin Holt set up the Operations Centre, while Billy Gammon and Dave Mans occupied a room at the South Camp Inn to unpack all the food supplies and prepare individual day bags for each crew member. There were 960 meals and 240 day bags. In total the food weighed 310kgs. There was more equipment and food on board than would have been required to row the Atlantic!

Tony Woodford, who knew Resolute well, sorted out the support boat and BBC filming boat, both of which would accompany *The Old Pulteney* for the first few days of the expedition. His job was made easier by the arrival of support boat skipper Will Stirling, a highly experienced polar mariner. They were soon checking over the only two suitable boats available in Resolute. Although they had been able to ask plenty of questions about these craft before arriving, it was the first time they had actually seen them.

The BBC's team, producer Matt Barrett and film-maker/oarsman Mark Beaumont, set about fitting the cameras to *The Old Pulteney* and checking the uplink system for transmitting material from the expedition.

Every working part required careful scrutiny to ensure it was in full working order.

The crews of *The Old Pulteney* and the two support boats also needed Arctic training, supervised by Tony Woodford. This included swimming in dry suits, understanding the drills for rescuing people from the water, knowing how to minimise the risks of hypothermia, and learning what to do in the event of a polar bear attack.

In fact the first polar bear encounter was in Resolute when a lone bear wandered too close to the town. It was a safe first sighting and filled everyone with an appreciation of how magnificent and dangerous these animals can be.

***Opposite (Clockwise)**: Preparing kit and supplies; Mark Beaumont checks camera equipment on the boat; Testing the expedition dry suits; Jock Wishart studies charts in the Operations Room.*

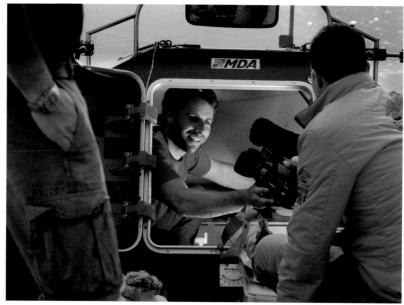

DEPARTURE

On Friday 29th July, the Operations Room buzzed from an early hour. The weather forecast told the team that a low pressure to the south over Hudson Bay, and a high to the west, put us in a northeasterly airstream, with clear skies. The warm temperatures in Resolute were close to a record seasonal high.

Jock Wishart recalls: "It was a great forecast and good enough for me to commit to setting out. High tide was about midday, so I told everyone to be ready to go that morning. In the Operations Room, there was a sense of apprehension, so I walked outside to gather my thoughts."

"At nine o'clock the team had a final briefing. I started with some facts. I pointed out that nothing was guaranteed...that no one has ever attempted anything like this before. I told them I knew I had the best possible crew, skilled oarsmen and expert mariners....a magnificent team. I also read the poem *The Quitter* by Robert Service and a few words my brother David, a former marine, had written to me. My final words were 'If it is possible, I have total confidence you can pull it off'.

"There was a heavy moment as my speech ended, followed by a few jibes about my sense of drama, and then we loaded the truck and headed down to the shoreline to board *The Old Pulteney*. With a few of our friends from Resolute watching on, but in remarkable stillness, we pulled out into the bay on our voyage into the unknown."

"If it is possible, I have total confidence you can pull it off."

Top: *Jock Wishart makes a final speech before the Expedition begins.*
Bottom: *Final Call - before setting out from Resolute Bay.*

UNDERWAY

It was assumed that from the start the crew would face fairly bumpy seas with fragments of sea ice. So, it seemed strange to everyone on-board to row the boat smoothly out of Resolute Bay on a mill-pond sea, with excellent visibility, dressed only in T-shirts. If it was easy, it was not for long: after three hours the boat reached a dense area of ice. With Jock Wishart at the helm, they bumped their way through it, crashing into one block of ice after another, dodgem car style until they reached open water once again.

This first encounter was followed by a dose of the Arctic's other surprise - mist and fog - with visibility down to only a few yards and a sense of total disorientation. It was like being in a refrigerator and Jock, who was steering, was soon shivering violently with the cold.

Nevertheless, the boat followed the coastline of Cornwallis Island, passing the planned overnight haven which was full of ice, before finding another place to shelter. They had covered about 20 nautical miles.

There was one more early warning to come, later on the first night. After their first expedition meal, everyone settled for the night leaving Billy to keep a lonely watch. Jock joined him to do a satellite phone interview with BBC Radio Four's *Today* programme about midnight. As he spoke to them, the boat became enveloped by sea ice which had drifted into the bay. Mark Delstanche realised the danger and, as the ice continued to pile in around *The Old Pulteney* and pulled hard on her anchor, he quickly donned his dry suit and leapt into the water to untangle the anchor and avoid disaster.

As Billy Gammon reported at the time: "The icebergs are the most extraordinary things – on the one hand so beautiful, yet lurking beneath this beauty lies a very real and very potent danger."

Top: *The Old Pulteney hits a bank of fog. Cornwallis Island.*
Bottom: *Calm waters leaving Resolute Bay .*

TO DEVON ISLAND

The voyage began as planned, edging along the south east edge of Cornwallis Island. The crew then expected to wait for the right weather to cross the Wellington Channel. This passage would be a real test for the crew, crossing open water in what were expected to be difficult conditions. The channel has a treacherous reputation, with a dominant northerly wind blowing down broken ice.

Once the boat left the relative shelter of Cornwallis Island, it would be a long and exposed passage to Devon Island, sixty miles to the east. After the crossing, *The Old Pulteney* would be able to pick a route northwards along the coastline. Everyone wanted to get on with it, expecting an adrenalin rush of a row.

As it happened a high pressure system arrived bringing with it light winds and calm, ice free seas. Jock seized the opportunity to make a dash for it, commenting to the crew that it was, "too good not to go for it!" So began 36 hours of non-stop rowing, in three hours shifts at the oars.

Left to right: *Rowing towards the Wellington Channel in benign conditions; The first bolt hole; In open waters; Mark Delstanche secures the boat with shifting ice around the boat.*

The channel has a treacherous reputation with a dominant northerly wind blowing down broken ice.

Dave Mans recalls: "It was a quite exhilarating night. We barely stopped for breath, always aware that conditions could change at any moment…. and with ruthless speed. We arrived, tired but ecstatic that the first potentially hazardous hurdle had been conquered."

After making landfall at Cape Daniell, it took them time to find a haven to pull up the boat onto the shore and rest. But the first big challenge was complete.

SUPPORT BOAT

Since *The Old Pulteney* left Resolute it had been followed by two support boats provided by local residents. Randy Nungaq (an engineer from the airport) and his brother Stephen were prepared to take the risk of making the trip across to Devon Island with their two small boats. For them it was a rare opportunity to venture out on the water in the short summer season. Both of these boats had good engines and were in reasonable condition. With expert skippers, they were capable of making the first leg, providing there was not too much ice on the first part of the journey.

One boat was a floating platform for the BBC. Documentary producer Matt Barrett was filming extra material from outside the boat. The second small boat was for the expedition's own support team. It was on hand in case there were any teething troubles. Skippering the two boats were Justin Holt and Will Stirling.

By August 1st, four days into the expedition, *The Old Pulteney* was well up the coast of Devon Island and the support boats needed to turn back to Resolute.

Their time following the boat had been in fairly calm conditions. This was in stark contrast to their return journey, which was hampered by strong winds, poor visibility and rough seas. Winds rose from a gusty 31km/hour to an almost impossible 70km/hour. They eventually made it back with fuel running low, and Randy and Stephen Nungaq finding themselves to be local heroes.

Now that *The Old Pulteney* crew had waved off their escorts, they really were alone. Survival was now in their own hands with no support, and no real chance of assistance should they get into difficulties.

Top: A support boat off Devon Island; **Bottom:** *Shotgun training in Resolute;* **Opposite:** *A polar bear approaches the tent on Devon Island.*

BEAR SCARE

Along the coastline of Devon Island the crew encountered four bears in a single day. They were patrolling the shoreline for basking seals. In summer the bears cannot hunt out on the ice, making them increasingly dangerous to humans.

At one overnight mooring, Dave Mans and Mark Beaumont decided to pitch one of the tents on the shore where they planned to get a more comfortable night's sleep than they could ever hope to get on the boat. With everyone settled for the night, Billy Gammon stayed up writing. Suddenly, in the corner of his eye, he saw a bear rapidly approaching the tent.

> *"As I looked out of the cabin I saw a large white furry animal fast approaching the tent. It was a polar bear."*

"I burst out the cabin beating my chest and yelling at the top of my voice, 'Whoa bear, whoa bear'. The bear didn't stop, turning instead towards the boat itself. Rob Sleep jumped out and cracked off several bear flares, which sent the bear lumbering off. Dave and Mark emerged from the tent, ashen-faced, and quickly clambered back onto *The Old Pulteney*. Less comfortable, but safer."

As Jock Wishart reflects: "Polar bears are dangerous creatures and you have to give them complete respect. If you come face-to-face with a polar bear, the first thing to do is watch for its body language...how it moves its head and shoulders. Polar bears don't make false charges. The safest thing to do is to start backing slowly away as far as you can and, if necessary, fire off a 'banger'. It usually scares the bear off."

UP THE COAST OF DEVON ISLAND

The route north followed the west coast of Devon Island and, with little or no ice, the only thing regulating progress was the weather.

The temperature had by now dropped significantly and with fairly strong winds on some days. Making headway was slow and physically tiring.

On some days, there was no option but to wait for conditions to improve, as any assault on the next leg of the expedition would have been pointless. Surprisingly, the greatest hazards were closer to shore, when strong winds made manoeuvring between floating ice too treacherous.

When the crew did row, the boredom of idle days was soon forgotten and they revelled in seeing beluga whales follow the boat and take in the stark grandeur of the scenery. By August 7th the crew had made it to the top of the Wellington Channel and were ready to make their move around the Grinnell Peninsula. Here, it was expected that the currents could pack ice into the narrower channel and make progress difficult.

Top: *Rob Sleep filling his day flask;*
Bottom: *Jock Wishart making a call to the Operations Room in Resolute.*

ROUTINES

Daily routines quickly became established on *The Old Pulteney*. Six people living on a small boat make routine essential, but also give each day a structure when so much else is unpredictable.

The arrival of the daily weather and ice bulletins from the Support Team were hugely important. Downloading them and absorbing the information was the serious starting point for every day. These overnight bulletins, along with calls made each morning and evening to the Operations Room in Resolute, shaped the day. It was important that the crew made contact on time to reassure the Ops Room that everything was OK.

Apart from discussing the weather and expedition details, speaking to people beyond the 'Arctic bubble' helped keep spirits up. Even trivial news from the outside world became important, especially at the low points of the expedition.

After breakfast every morning Rob Sleep, Mark Delstanche and Jock Wishart discussed the plan for the day. This was shared with everyone to be sure the whole team supported their decisions. It was also the time when any issues or concerns could be raised.

However, it was hunger that drove most other routines. Apart from the large amounts of energy needed to row, the cold demanded a high calorie intake too. Meals and food fast became key elements of the day and huge topics of conversation and banter. Breakfast and evening meals were highlights in each day. The rituals around setting up the stove, sorting the food rations and then sitting down to eat were major events, and great morale boosters. Satisfied stomachs fuelled positive minds.

Amongst the rations were some meals more prized than others. Some of the dry food packs were universally considered to be little more than animal fodder, but still eaten. To Billy Gammon, other packs were devoured like prize gourmet meals. "With so much at stake, we decided to run a 'lucky dip' selection process at every meal. Over the course of the expedition we came up with a number of lotto variations to distribute the food - making a huge drama out of each meal time."

It was the same pot-luck approach for distributing the 'day bags' for snacking that were essential to maintain energy levels. Gloating was rife and barter was frequent: 'dog treats' were swapped for pretzels, and haribo sharks swapped for nuts. Anyone with jelly snakes was viewed with envy!

More often than not, meals were eaten on the shore. Dave Mans was chief cook, drawing on his army experience to transform even the most challenging of meals (dehydrated omelette) into an edible feast.

"We took it in turns to begin with" Billy Gammon admits, "but it fast became obvious that Dave was a master chef, so the rest of us opted for other duties, like harvesting the ice we needed to melt as our water supply, as quite often we could not use the water maker. It was, after all, the only other vital ingredient!"

"With food as our focus, we'd invariably chat about the highs and lows of the day, plans for tomorrow and comment about the progress we were making."

Some of the dry food packs were universally considered to be little more than animal fodder, but still eaten.

FIRST ICE CHALLENGE

The Sheills Peninsula juts out from the west side of Devon Island towards Bathurst Island, with the Penny Straits to the north. From this point onwards the crew would be on constant alert for sea ice floes. Their best assets were the ice reports from Kim Partington, who was studying satellite images of the area from MDA. These reports, along with the weather forecasts from Chris Tibbs, gave the crew an indication of what lay ahead.

There were two dangers: floating ice in the channel itself which could damage the boat and her rudder; and the risk of ice filling the bays that they relied on for shelter. If the bays were inaccessible, the boat would be exposed to the perils of fast moving ice in the main channel. Ice might also be a problem if it moved in whilst the crew were hiding from the elements, making an escape to open water impossible.

Negotiating the Penny Straits was the most dangerous leg of the route so far. A tactical mistake could be costly. Once through the straits there would be some options for the middle section of the voyage. One thing was in their favour. According to Billy Gammon, "because we'd made swift progress to this point, there was less pressure to push ahead. We could afford to wait for the right moment."

On August 8th, with 48 hours of good weather forecast, the moment seemed right to attack the Straits challenge, and get as far north as possible before the winds changed.

Jock Wishart decided to miss out one stop-over, and simply plough on up the coast towards a place called Hungry Bay. It was about 30 miles away. His plan was a calculated risk: to push hard, then rest up before an even more daunting passage round the Grinnell Peninsula. The north-northwesterly winds would help clear out any ice blocking the route.

Jock insisted on stopping to visit Barrow Point - where a cairn stands in Sir John Barrow's name. As Secretary of State at the British Admiralty he had promoted Arctic exploration by pioneers such as by John Ross, William Edward Parry and John Franklin to venture into the far north. From its high vantage point there was a breathtaking view of what seemed like the entire Arctic North. It was bathed in bright sunshine and stretched in every direction for as far as the eye could see.

As Billy reported: "There, in front of us, lay two very different sides to the Arctic - on the one hand calm turquoise water, and on the other some extremely menacing looking ice fields...which we knew we'd shortly have to navigate through."

Speaking on the satellite phone Jock Wishart told the Operations Team: "Something is really happening up here. Even last year, we could not have expected something like this. We're in amongst some ice floes here, but nothing like as big as some we saw earlier today which, I have to say, were positively dangerous and were moving at some speed. Here in the shallow water of this bay any big ones will pass us by. What gobsmacks me is that we're seeing so much open water so far north so early in August. I hadn't expected it."

With a smooth row to Hungry Bay, the next target was Spit Island. They'd cleared the Penny Straits and were at the north end of Devon Island. This was a major moment. In terms of miles, it was the half-way point of the voyage. The hardest part was yet to come, but reaching this point so quickly was remarkable.

The Penny Straits was the most dangerous leg of the route so far.

Opposite: *The first encounters with ice approaching the Grinnell Peninsula.*

ICEBOUND

After the Penny Straits, the team took a well-deserved breather just beyond a landmark called Napier Bay. From a hill above their anchorage they could survey what lay ahead of them. After 12 days, and ahead of schedule, the crew were facing the next big leg of the voyage. Straight in front of them was the Grinnell Peninsula, the gateway to the whole of the northerly part of the route. Beyond it lay Ellef Ringnes Island and the 1996 position of the Magnetic North Pole.

Rob Sleep, Jock Wishart, Dave Mans and Mark Delstanche had clambered to a high point and returned with news that there was a lot more ice ahead between the Grinnell Peninsula and Exmouth Island. It was the bottleneck of ice Jock had been warned about. Despite the observations it was agreed that a way through could be found.

After six hours heaving on the oars however, there was a dramatic change. The channel closed and the navigable leads through the ice quickly narrowed. As Jock reported: "For hours on end we aimlessly followed the leads, looking for the open water. All the time the ice was converging, slowly suffocating *The Old Pulteney*."

As the situation worsened, the pressure on the helmsman to find an escape route intensified. The Arctic was tightening its grip and squeezing the life out of the crew, the boat and the expedition.

"It was a pretty frightening experience" according to Billy Gammon. "The noise of the ice crashing up against the hull was deafening and with each blow *The Old Pulteney* let out another shriek of pain. It was agonising to hear and desperately worrying."

This was the Arctic at its most brutal. It was overwhelmingly powerful and there was little the crew could do. The mood on deck quietened as the seriousness of the situation hit home. Progress became more erratic and the objective of reaching Exmouth Island was ditched. Reaching safety was all that counted.

"With one final shudder from the converging ice we finally ground to a halt, with nowhere to turn." Billy says. Everyone knew this spelled real trouble. "At that moment we were faced with the prospect of having to try and haul *The Old Pulteney* out on to the ice to avoid being crushed. Given the ice formation this would have been a huge challenge, but it was fast looking like our only option."

Whilst the grim reality was being absorbed, almost as quickly as the ice had enveloped them, it began to open up again, revealing a maze of leads and more open water. It was a lifeline and the crew grabbed it with a real sense of urgency to get clear of trouble.

Finally, after more than seventy miles of struggle, and thirty six hours of exertion, the boat reached land, back at the place they had begun and, though no one said it, where they should have stayed all those hours before.

"The noise of the ice crashing up against the hull was deafening"

Top: *The shore was a chance to escape the cramped boat;*
Bottom: *Mark Delstanche at the helm and Dave Mans rowing.*

WEATHER OR NOT?

It took another 24 hours to round the top of the Grinnell Peninsula. It was clear that, with ice now ever present, progress relied on careful judgment and interpreting the weather and satellite data. Details were closely scrutinized and, behind every decision to forge ahead, was a long discussion about the options, risks and rewards.

To escape from a landfall on the Northern coast of Devon Island just East of Napier Bay the crew had to wait two days for a change in wind direction, and for the currents to move the ice out of the way. The temperature dropped markedly in a northerly wind and night temperatures dropped to around zero. It was little warmer during the day.

When the conditions did change the crew made headway in ice-strewn seas, but only eastwards to Cape Ogle ten miles further on. With poor visibility, it was only possible to get a good view of the surrounding sea. These glimpses seemed only to confirm that the ice trap was set to hold fast for some time. There was no option but to wait it out.

With regular checks continuing from different vantage points, eventually a clear view of an opening through the ice to the north east was spotted and the relatively short crossing to Table Island could be made. Now, navigation required serious concentration from the helmsman. For the first time, there were towering icebergs and ribbons of tightly packed ice, with belts of open water between them. For all the challenges such obstacles provided, it was the better of two possible routes. It was longer, heading eastwards to take in Cornwall Island and Amund Ringnes Island, but it avoided a riskier direct crossing to Ellef Ringnes Island. Taking that course could have led to serious difficulties in a completely exposed channel with no bolt holes.

Whether it was good luck or good timing, Table Island was reached just as more fog descended. It meant a further wait, but at least there was a sense that everyone's patience had paid off. The boat was free from the biggest threat they'd encountered so far and had moved forwards again.

SURVEYING

The extreme remoteness of the Arctic makes any scientific work difficult and expensive. Field work expeditions to the region are few and far between. Working with the National Oceanography Centre at Southampton University, the *Old Pulteney Row To The Pole* expedition was able to undertake valuable survey work.

Dave Mans, who had studied oceanography at Southampton, was the ideal choice to be the expedition's field scientist. His main study used a special CTD probe which was plunged into the water on the end of a 100 metre line to capture data on water salinity and temperature at different depths.

Because the waters in this part of the Canadian Archipelago have only just begun to be ice free, it was an early opportunity for Dr. Simon Boxall from Southampton University to understand what is happening in this area. Sea ice, which loses its salinity over time, is melting, and Boxall is studying how this may be affecting the water just beneath the surface. If it leads to a 'freshening' of the water it might accelerate the speed of ice melt.

The shallow draught of the rowing boat hardly disturbed the water, making it ideal for sampling. The readings, taken daily, extended along the entire 500 mile length of the journey. Ultimately, it would be one data set, but with the possibility of others venturing through these waters in future, the results make a valuable 'base line' study.

In rowing through a pristine wilderness the crew had a privileged view of the Arctic's permanent residents. The bolt holes they chose were often popular places for walruses and seals to bask on the ice debris strewn over the water. Onshore they had encounters with Arctic foxes, wolves and polar bears.

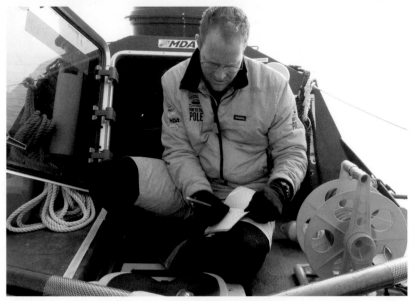

This page: *Dave prepares the CTD survey equipment.*
Opposite: *Wilderness residents.*

BOAT LIFE

The cramped conditions on *The Old Pulteney* should have made tensions inevitable. The boat was really too small for its crew of six, but was ingeniously designed to at least offer sleeping berths and storage for all the kit and just enough essentials to be a viable vessel for the expedition.

It was remarkable that after three weeks there had been virtually no clashes. Being able to get off the boat some nights and find personal space on a long walk, or sleep in the tent, made all the difference.

The crew had undergone Belbin team profiling tests, under the tutelage of Trevor Laurence, before leaving the UK. These had highlighted some crew dynamics that could either lead to extraordinary success or, just as likely, disaster. Taking this, and a number of other recommendations into consideration, the crew was split, creating two 'watches'. These became close teams, and each group of three worked effectively during the voyage.

The other significant by-product to come out of the research was the decision for Jock to step back from daily skippering duties, leaving those to Rob Sleep and Mark Delstanche. It meant Jock to devote his time to the overall expedition strategy, and removed the potential for crew frustrations and dissent which could have arisen from having a single decision-maker.

In reality, most expedition decisions were shared and aired and this fostered a strong sense of camaraderie.

If there were tensions, they were mostly about the little things. Jock was singled out for his loud snoring and when everyone slept onboard, the claustrophobic cabins, especially the 'coffin' berths, made for restless nights.

"It was the long days marooned with little to do but idle time away with card games that were hardest to deal with" according to Rob Sleep. "You know there is probably nothing you can do about it, but some of the guys did begin to question if the cautious approach was the right one. When you have a boat full of athletes, telling them to do nothing is not easy."

Claustrophobic cabins, especially the 'coffin' berths, made for restless nights.

BREAKOUT, BREAKTHROUGH

Dogged by poor weather, Table Island was home for two long days. "From the cliffs on the island we could see open water lay beyond the ice packed around the coast. All we needed was a change in wind direction to force an opening and we'd be away." Jock was beginning to form a dramatic change to his plan. "There has been time to study the satellite images and talk through our plan for the days ahead. If conditions were right, I decided we should make a massive push across the Belcher Channel to Cornwall Island before heading on to Ellef Ringnes. It meant rowing a distance of seventy nautical miles, our biggest single haul so far. But the rewards would be enormous. When the fog finally lifted on August 17th we could see the opening we'd been looking for and shortly after breakfast everything was packed back onto the boat and she eased away towards Cornwall Island."

It was now bitterly cold. The air temperature was -2°C, but the wind chill meant it felt considerably colder. It didn't affect the performance of the crew. If anything, the chill only increased the work rate. After a short refuelling stop at Cornwall Island, the huge long row began across waters that were largely ice-free.

"We met a couple of lively pack ice fields" Mark Delstanche remembers. "Most of the crew had become adept at avoiding collisions, so it was a bit of a surprise when Mark Beaumont steered us at full speed square on to a big piece of ice. There was a thunderous crack and, with hindsight, it was amazing we escaped without damaging the hull. If nothing else Mark had upstaged our most accomplished 'berg-hitter, Captain 'Iceberg' Wishart, whose unerring eye could be relied on to bump into anything in our way."

The boat weaved in and out of the pack ice on the crossing and, twenty five hours after leaving Table Island, they reached Ellef Ringnes Island. They had rowed continuously for most of that time, in three hour shifts, catching sleep whenever they could. The day was not yet over, not by a long way.

"There was a thunderous crack...it was amazing we escaped without damaging the hull."

ICE FLOES AND A SAFE HAVEN

After reaching the coast of Ellef Ringnes, they pushed further north to find a suitable bolt hole, only to be confronted by a mass of jumbled ice. They scouted and probed to find a way through, but it was an impenetrable wall which seemed endless. Needing a safe place to stop, they carried on for a further eleven difficult, dangerous, hours without success. Eventually, giving up, they diverted west to reach the relative safety of King Christian Island. Despite the end, it had been a sensational and exhilarating thirty six hours. Whilst almost totally exhausted, they had rowed eighty nautical miles and manoeuvred to within fifty miles of the finish at the 1996 Magnetic North Pole.

It had been a sensational and exhilarating 36 hours

Opposite: *The crew head away from Table Island* **Top:** *Rowing a wide lead;* **Bottom:** *Pushing the boat to shore*

THOR ISLAND

"We are so near and yet so far" Billy Gammon wrote on the expedition blog. "You feel like you can almost see it!"

After an overnight stay on King Christian Island, the crew had ventured further north again to Thor Island. With the preferred passage around the east side blocked, they had found a reasonable anchorage to the west.

Weariness really caught up with everyone now. Adrenalin had kept them going, now it was time to recharge and recover. Waking to freezing temperatures again, they discovered the area had filled with ice. It was heavily packed in and it was clear there would be no rowing for several days. Chris Tibbs, the expedition weather forecaster advised that there was no point attempting anything for at least two days because strong winds blowing hard from the northwest would make conditions impossible, and highly dangerous.

No one liked the idea of another enforced stop, but there were no complaints. The expedition was now further north than had been expected after only three weeks, and they were ideally positioned for the final assault. If they had learned anything, it was to work with the weather, not fight it. There were some big decisions ahead, but no one doubted that, when it came to it, Jock with Mark Delstanche and Rob Sleep to advise him, had an unerring ability to make the right call. Whilst insisting on waiting earlier in the expedition had seemed over cautious, the strategy had resulted in dramatic progress.

Top: *Large icebergs off Ellef Ringnes Island.*
Bottom: *Ice just off shore at Thor Island;* **Opposite:** *The sun dips, but never sets in the Arctic summer.*

ANXIOUS TIMES

The weather which battered Thor Island lasted several days. Despite being ahead of schedule, as time went on, the possibility that they may not get any further began to gnaw away and put doubts in the crew's minds .

The biggest concern was that with every day the end of the summer came nearer. In the Arctic, this is the point when the ice begins to form again. A prolonged delay could scupper the chance to attempt the last leg to Deer Bay, and '96 Pole. Each day the forecast proved accurate. There was no let up in the weather. Worse, the direction of the prevailing wind was pushing ice into the path they knew they had have to take.

No one said it, but amongst the support team there was a sense that Thor Island might mark the end of the expedition. Kim Partington, the ice expert, was looking at MDA's satellite images and finding it hard to be optimistic about the expedition's prospects. He told the support team, but not the crew, that in his opinion the chance of getting round to the Pole position was no greater than 30 percent, unless there was more encouraging news from the boat.

There was a sense that Thor Island might mark the end of the expedition.

EYE IN THE SKY

For days the team sat looking across Dome Bay towards the headland of the Noice Peninsula. It was the most frustrating waiting game of the whole expedition. There was a strong sense amongst the crew that they should be moving on. Everyone realised that the number of days they had left before the ice re-froze were ticking by.

They could see a fracture through the pack ice which ran parallel to the coast of the Noice shoreline, and there were discussions about whether this could be explored. The argument against this was that leads can close as easily as they open up.

Everything seemed to hang on Chris Tibbs weather report. On August 23rd the wind had changed to an easterly which, they hoped, would blow the ice away from the coastline. Detailed ice observations were gathered by the crew from different positions on Thor Island and re-layed back to Kim Partington in Britain. A RADARSAT-2 satellite image from MDA had shown the distribution of ice in phenomenal detail throughout the voyage, showing where it was thin and breaking up. Adding intelligence from the crew at this critical moment would complete the picture.

By August 24th the winds which had blown at a steady 20 knots from the east were due to weaken to 10 knots, making it possible to contemplate an attempt to leave their 'prison island'. Kim Partington's team at Polar Imaging fed information back to the boat showing a lot of ice in the wrong places but, as everyone knew, the situation can change quickly, so everyone was put on standby to move.

Of more immediate concern, was a stream of ice coming directly towards Thor Island which was in danger of trapping them.

Top: *Harvesting ice to supply water on Thor Island;* *Bottom:* *MDA image of the ice at Thor Island and Noice Peninsula - August 24th 2011;* *Opposite:* *Ice floes passing the camp at Thor Island.*

HEY BABY!

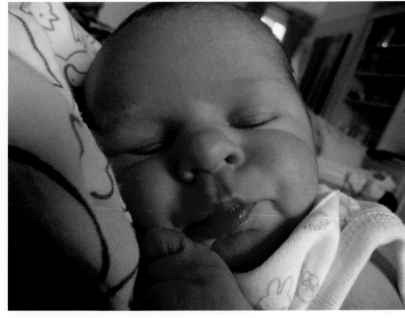

For all the frustrations about the weather reports from the Support Team, it was not all bad news from Britain. Mark Delstanche had been waiting to hear from his partner Helene who was expecting their first child. They had decided he could not pass the chance to be part of the *Old Pulteney Row To The Pole* expedition, even though he would miss the birth.

Keeping in reasonably regular contact made it a little easier, but Mark was as anxious as any new father. News of the birth came through on Thor Island, prompting a riot of celebrations.

Mark wrote his son a letter and left it in a cairn he built on the island. "I wanted to express a few of my hopes and feelings about him and his future. Hopefully the advice that I left in the letter will stand my son in good stead for his future. Mind you, if he ever goes to gets the letter, he might prefer to find a map and compass which only points South. It would be more useful!"

Junior wasn't given a name until Mark returned to share the moment with Helene 10 days later. "I guess junior is going to have quite a story to tell about his entry into the world when he's older."

*Left: New dad Mark celebrates with Jock Wishart; **Right:** Junior;*
***Opposite:** A team portrait.*

NOICE DAY!

The four days of waiting were over. Jock Wishart at first directed the boat to head out of the way of the incoming ice. Once they were out and moving it was clearer that conditions were not too bad.

"I turned to the guys and said, 'Look, why don't we go for it and see if we can struggle across? At least we might get across to the south side of the Noice Peninsula.' Everyone agreed. It was a real case of pumping ourselves up and putting faith in the saying *who dares wins*."

Little by little the weather was improving and by the time they reached the Noice side of Dome Bay, it was a beautiful sunny evening. More miraculously, the wind cleared the ice in front of them like a pathway. It was almost beckoning them to push on.

The Operations Room in Resolute was plotting their progress on a tracking beacon as it moved steadily in a northwest direction. Richard Webster reported that there appeared to be a small ice blockage ahead, but nothing that looked insurmountable. Suddenly, it really looked as if the break out and final push had been successful.

By late evening Jock was able to send a message reporting a huge surge forwards: "I now stand here, probably only 18 miles from the finish on the west coast of the Noice Peninsula, which we always thought would be the most difficult and dangerous part of the whole expedition…the final part. And yet it is like a gateway has been made for us and we're taking full advantage of it."

Top: Wolf, Thor Island; ***Top Right:*** *Rowing into open water, Noice Peninsula;* ***Bottom Right:*** *On ice watch rounding Noice;* ***Bottom left:*** *Jock after entering Deer Bay.*

They continued rowing through the night. It was fairly open water right to the entrance to Deer Bay and only ten miles from the Pole position. Jock estimated it would only take three to four hours to cover the remaining distance. Surprised by the progress, the UK office requested they slow down to buy them time to prepare for the expected media interest.

On *The Old Pulteney*, no one could quite believe their luck. It was premature, but the crew began mentally celebrating the completion of their journey. Everything looked set for success.

The wind blew and cleared the ice in front of them like a pathway.
It was almost beckoning them to push on.

IN IT FOR THE LONG HAUL

Not far into Deer Bay the boat began to meet more ice. At first this seemed to be no more challenging than other ice floes they had encountered. As time passed, it became more densely packed. Finally, after hours searching for a route through, they were confronted by a complete blockage. The ice was also backed up behind them, slowly but surely boxing them in until they were surrounded with nowhere to turn.

As Billy Gammon reflected: "You can hardly imagine the emotional impact on us all, knowing how close we were to the end but trapped by this impenetrable mass of ice. It was hugely disheartening. We were facing failure after 498 miles...and only two miles short of the end."

Already fatigued by the overnight row and the tussle with the ice, the team clambered out of the boat. Their only option now was to pull the boat out of the water and haul it across the ice.

"It was extraordinary, now I think back to that moment" says Jock. "Everyone seemed to accept that, however hard it was going to be, we'd got to drag the boat the last two miles. Not finishing was inconceivable. The boat had runners so it could be hauled over the ice like a giant sledge, but it was going to be a brutal physical challenge. All we really knew was that staying where we were was out of the question. It was simply too dangerous."

So, the routines they had practiced in the early part of the expedition were put into practise. At over 900 kilos fully laden, *The Old Pulteney* was not easily raised out of the water. Poles were attached either side of the bow and with pulleys, inflatable rollers and a lot of human muscle, she was converted from boat to sledge.

Jock managed a hurried call to the Operations Room, sounding anxious. He said only "It's a struggle." It was a classic understatement. The ice was far from being a flat surface. There were huge ice hillocks, long stretches of ice rubble and crumbling ice leads to cross, meaning progress was painfully slow. The boat was heaved in and out of small ice breaks, which at least provided some respite, but more obstacles faced them on the other side of each short stretch of the water.

For all the consideration of this kind of challenge when designing the boat, no one in the crew had actually done this before. Billy Gammon called it "one of the most arduous tasks I have ever faced."

For what seemed like endless hours they fought on. This was no skirmish, as previous difficulties had been. This was full on combat.

"We were facing failure after 498 miles... and only two miles short of the end"

***Opposite:** Slow, backbreaking work for the last two miles.*

"It was as if the Arctic was trying to make a point" according to Dave Mans. "Worse than that, as we neared the end we began to experience more ice drift, so when we felt we were almost there a check on our positioning system revealed we had in fact floated further away."

Eventually, with a final frustration-fuelled effort, *The Old Pulteney* was pulled hard across some ice and down a slope into water – at the Pole's position. They had arrived. Not as they had imagined, but at the finishing line.

"It was almost too much effort to celebrate, so our cheers were fairly muted. No one had any energy left. We were simply relieved to be there" says Billy Gammon.

It may have been Jock Wishart's idea, his expedition, but as the last few miles had proved, success was a team effort of enormous proportions.

Their first call was to the support team in Resolute Bay. It was 6.30 in the evening local time (0130 BST). "Guys, we're there. We've made it. We're at the '96 Mag. Pole!" The ice crossing had taken almost ten hours and it was more than thirty six hours since they left their original bolt hole on Thor Island.

Utterly exhausted, they had given everything to do it. All anyone wanted now was sleep. Leaving the boat where she was in the water, everyone clambered into the cabins, took off their yellow dry suits and fell into their sleeping bags.

This was no skirmish, as previous difficulties had been. This was full on combat.

Right: *Coaxing The Old Pulteney through a short stretch of water;*
Opposite: *Prizing the boat onto the ice.*

THE 96!

There was not a great deal of opportunity to get a good rest. Media interviews were flooding in and satellite calls with broadcasters meant Jock barely had time to sleep before he was being awoken to speak about their achievement. First up was BBC Radio 4's *Today* p rogramme. Summoning up more energy than he expected, he told presenter Justin Webb: "It was the most incredible journey and I suppose it will go down in history as the first time anyone has been able to row to a Pole position. It's a real, true, global first."

It was the first time any of the team had been asked to put the achievement in any kind of context. It was also true. The *Old Pulteney Row To The Pole* success was a genuine 'first': no one had rowed in these waters before and there is no historical record of any boat being rowed to a Pole position.

This first interview was picked up by other media, not all of them hearing what was intended. Jock had told Justin Webb that "At the very last moment King Neptune tried to get his own back and he gave us a real bite on the bum to remind us we were still human. Having to pull the boat over the ice and the rubble and through the leads, that was a really hard reminder to us that we are mortals." By the time Daily Telegraph had filed their story, readers were told that a seal called King Neptune had actually bitten him on his bottom!

After a few hours of sleep to recharge the batteries, Jock set up camp in the bow cabin for a string of interviews with journalists. Meanwhile, Mark Beaumont was also working away on sending his reports back to the BBC and their website.

For several hours neither of them could move as excitement about their story grew.

News of the success sent hits on the expedition's own website soaring and downloads of the short video clips of the boat-hauling and the moment they arrived at the Pole were viewed by thousands.

In reaching the 1996 position of the Magnetic North Pole the expedition had demonstrated in a striking way that the annual summer ice melt was accelerating. Simply by taking the boat all the way, they had shown how vulnerable the region is to changes in the climate.

"Having to pull over the ice and the rubble and through the leads, that was a really hard reminder to us that we are mortals."

Left: *The crew celebrates;* **Centre:** *Lost in the ice;* **Right:** *At the '96 certified position of the Magnetic North Pole.*

ON TO SAFETY

Their sense of glory would not last long. The journey was not over yet. So, whilst more media interviews were conducted, fuelled by coffee and tea, Dave Mans and Mark Delstanche went off to 'recce' the area around the pole position to see how they could extract themselves from the middle of the pack ice.

The certified position of the Magnetic North Pole is in fairly deep water and nowhere near land. There was no alternative to ploughing on, however tough it may be, to reach the coast of Ellef Ringnes Island. There, the boat could be beached, pulled well clear of the waterline and the crew could walk to a landing strip to be airlifted back to Resolute Bay far to the south.

"At this stage land, no matter where, was our priority" Mark Delstanche explains. "We returned with news that the leads had increased, but that we were still ice locked. We sketched a proposed route, but as we'd learned yesterday, most of it would have to be decided as we traveled. The reality was the job today was going to be a tough one."

The last hour at the Pole was spent taking 'victory' photos, then it was on with the day job. The extraction point was 40 nautical miles away, and the sooner they found a way to the safety of the coast, nearer to the landing strip, the better. With the boat packed and dry suits on once more the boat was on the move again.

"Whilst the horizon looked more promising, what was noticeable was the rate at which the water was freezing" Billy commented. "The leads from yesterday hadn't vanished as the ice compressed, they had started to freeze. In some places what had been free flowing water was now 25-30mm of ice. The Arctic freeze had begun at exactly the same time as we reached the Pole position. It was more proof of how lucky we'd been to get here so quickly. Days clearly counted."

The whole operation was not a precise science. Pick axes, pulleys and a brute force were applied to get the Old Pulteney moving.

After two hours cajoling the boat over the ice, they reached a big enough lead to float the boat. It looked like the best waterway towards land, although no one could really be confident. With a sweeping team ahead of the boat clearing out floating ice and debris, the boat moved a little faster. Mark Delstanche and Dave Mans took to the water, swimming ahead of the boat and using their arms to bash the thinner ice to break a route through. It was heroic to even consider it in the bitter cold.

After wading, whacking and winding along the narrow lead they reached a bigger stretch of open water, and eventually it was wide enough to put the oars in the water. Rob Sleep took the helm, wrapped up against the plummeting temperatures and constant breeze. "It took a few lusty blows with our oars to break us out, but at long last we were free of the ice. There was a massive cheer from the crew as we broke from the clutches of the suffocating ice field."

The last five miles to shore took three hours head on to a strong 20 knot wind. But, eventually a beach for landing was spotted and everyone stopped rowing to allow Jock, as expedition leader, to power the boat to its last resting place. He made an impromptu speech, telling the crew how proud he was to have reached this point, before pulling *The Old Pulteney* to the shore.

"The Arctic freeze had begun at exactly the same time as we reached the Pole position"

ABANDONED

From the boat's final resting place it was at least a 15 mile hike to an abandoned cold war base, Isachsen. It was built back in the 1940s as a radar base by the United States as part of what was called the DEW Line but was closed in the late 1970s. With a long landing strip, Isachsen is now only used occasionally by small Twin Otters and DC3 Basler aircraft which are the workhorses of the Arctic. Each year Kenn Borek Air builds small fuel caches at the strip for use in longer flights and for emergencies.

At the boat there was a considerable amount of equipment to strip out and pack ready to be lugged to the rendezvous. All six crew were to carry packs weighing up to 40 kilos for two separate hikes.

The terrain looked reasonable, but there were wide areas of cloying mud to cross, so progress was slow. Any hope of completing a return journey in one day quickly disappeared.

Speaking as he walked through the mud Billy Gammon commented with grave humour: "This is exactly what I wanted after 29 days at sea, a nice leisurely stroll. The good news is that when we get there we have to go back and do it again."

Isachsen is an eerie cold war ghost settlement. All the buildings, vehicles and equipment remain as they were left over thirty years ago. Because the original plan had been to go back to the boat after the first trip, the crew had only one sleeping bag, carried in case of an emergency. After wandering between the derelict buildings, they picked out a sleeping block to take shelter and improvised with mattresses to bed down on for the night. After making the return journey the next day, the crew had one last night on *The Old Pulteney*, before it was time to say a last farewell to the boat. She had proved to be such a massive part of their expedition, and they were saying goodbye to an old friend.

"What an amazing, extraordinary vessel" Jock says. "We knew what we wanted her to do and she delivered it all! She was bumped, bashed, battered by rough weather and finally pulled over miles of ice, never once letting us down."

The Old Pulteney would be left where she sat, high on the shore to face everything the Arctic has to throw at her over the winter and summer. She may even offer shelter to other visitors.

Eight hours after waving goodbye to the boat, the crew arrived at Isachsen for a second and final night. The satellite phone was playing up, but eventually a conversation with Kenn Borek Air was made calling in a flight. The last of the hard work had been done. A return to civilisation was imminent.

"We knew what we wanted her to do and she delivered it all!"

Left to right: The Old Pulteney is dragged to her final resting place; The long walk to Isachsen; Tough going approaching Isachsen - a wrecked plane in the distance; Home for the night in one of the derelict buildings at the old radar base.

EXTRACTION CAN BE PAINFUL

The final day began with falling snow and fog. It wasn't what the pilot wanted to hear. Landing would have been too dangerous. After a bit of reassurance from Jock that the weather was improving, the Twin Otter set out from Resolute on its three and a half hour flight, touching down at 11.40 in the morning.

"Getting off the plane to greet us was Richard Webster, the expedition's support team scientist and reserve oarsman. He brought a bottle of Old Pulteney donated by our title sponsor, so with a glass in hand, we toasted our good fortune and the expedition's end. We all smell horrific, look like Neanderthals and despite eating our 6,000 calories a day, seem to have lost a good few pounds" says Billy.

"There was a noticeable quiet amongst the crew during the flight, as our route retraced the steps we'd taken over the islands, ice blockades and open water. The landscape below had been our playground and tormentor for the past 32 days, and it was weird to be leaving."

Sitting on the plane, Jock Wishart looked completely exhausted. For him, it was a huge relief. His hair-brained idea, conceived in Resolute four years earlier, had been completed. He was returning there now as the first person to take a boat under human power to any Pole position. In reaching the '96 Magnetic North Pole his crew had achieved a journey without precedent. He had nothing left in his tank.

"We all smell horrific, look like Neanderthals and despite eating our 6,000 calories a day, seem to have lost a good few pounds."

Opposite: *An exhausted Jock on the flight back to Resolute;*
Above: *Mark Delstanche, Rob Sleep, Billy Gammon, Mark Beaumont, Jock Wishart and Dave Mans, Isachsen, August 31st 2011.*

REFLECTIONS

By Jock Wishart

Reaching the 1996 Magnetic North Pole marks a bittersweet moment. The *Old Pulteney Row To The Pole* expedition made it because the pace of melting in the Arctic summer is far greater than it once was. In a few years it may be relatively easy to row these waters if they become completely ice free. That may already be unavoidable, but it would be a tragedy to see this remarkable, vital, habitat change to such an extent.

Looking back now the expedition is over, I realize it taught me something important: that it is worth reaching for something, however far beyond us it may appear at first. To have shaped the expedition was a long journey in itself. To have found a team – far wider than my five rowing companions – and then worked alongside them has been a privilege. Shared passions for adventure, sports or the Arctic have driven this team to great heights. At times we have struggled and stumbled, but we have always known in exactly which direction we were heading.

My thanks go most of all to the amazing crew. Rob Sleep and Mark Delstanche were extraordinarily generous in their support to me. Mark Beaumont joined us to make a film for the BBC but rowed in our crew and was an essential part of it. Dave Mans brought science skills, rowing prowess and a quiet 'get on with it' approach to the expedition which was indispensable. Billy Gammon had already spent most of his energy fund raising before the voyage began. On the expedition he helped bring the entire team together with spirit and as our communicator, kept telling our story.

There were many letters, emails and social media comments which reached us on the expedition and on our return home. They were valued at the time, and appreciated now. In many other ways we have been welcomed back by others who followed our voyage. My thanks go to them all.

Since returning to Britain, I have been able to look at our journey and to compare the conditions we experienced in August 2011. It is now clear that we really must have had someone looking after us: completing the journey would have been impossible in 2009 or 2010. The weather and ice conditions in the area would have prevented it.

Marty Bergmann, the director of the Canadian government's Polar Continental Shelf Programme at Resolute, had told me in 2009 that he had no idea how they would rescue us if the boat was crushed. Bluntly, he told me I was mad. I would have enjoyed a conversation with him after our success. But sadly, he died in the Resolute plane crash just days before our expedition ended. He was a valued friend, as were several others killed in the tragedy.

Lastly, there are many, many people who have helped me and the *Old Pulteney Row To The Pole*. In fact, far too many to mention. Nevertheless, my heartfelt thanks go to them all for their encouragement, advice, ideas, energy, time and generosity.

In writing this book Rod Macrae has captured the essence of the story which I hope will be enjoyed by all who have a spirit of adventure and love of the Arctic.

Yours Aye,

Jock
November 2011